DO ELVES PLAY THE ELECTRIC GUITAR?

FUNNY THINGS HEARD IN GUITAR LESSONS

By Kaz Simmons

Do Elves Play the Electric Guitar?, by Kaz Simmons

Published by Fast Awake Ltd, 2021

ISBN: 978-1-3999-0890-0

Illustrations © Jamie Ogilvie-Forbes
Image on page 63 © Phillip Walton

Design and layout by Kaz Simmons and Toby Stockdale

Text copyright © Kaz Simmons 2021

Fast Awake Ltd
168 Church Road, Hove, BN3 2DL

www.kazsimmons.com

Printed and bound in the United Kingdom.

Contents

Introduction

As any parent or teacher knows all too well, kids can say the funniest things. I've been teaching guitar to children of all ages for the past 17 years, and I've heard my fair share of sweetly-voiced hilarity.

I'm not sure what prompted me to start taking note of their comments. At first I only wrote down the ones that were music related. But then it gradually extended to anything that made me laugh. Sometimes they would ramble delightfully on about something they were excited or worried about, or simply ponder as children do. And if their musings tickled me, I jotted them down.

Every July I would post the 'guitar funnies' on my private social media page (attributed anonymously of course), and when this became a tradition that friends would look forward to each year, I was urged to collate the quotes in a book.

The quotes are from 2013 to summer 2021. Some are from online lessons, due to the COVID-19 pandemic. This was a totally new way of teaching and learning that threw up some unique challenges and, with them, some quirky observations. At the time of writing, the world is still gripped by the fear and uncertainty of the pandemic, and revisiting all of these quotes has continually lifted my spirits and been an invaluable distraction.

As well as teaching guitar, I used to be a singer-songwriter, but gradually moved away from performing to focus on teaching full-time. I love the job and I adore my students, and I thank them all hugely for their contributions to this book and for giving me such incredible job satisfaction.

This book is dedicated to all my students, past and present.

The Guitar Lesson

Boy's first lesson.

Me: What music do you like?

Boy: I don't really like music.

I point to the bridge on the guitar.

Me: What's this?

Boy: I don't know.

Me: It's the bridge.

I point to the body of the guitar.

Me: What's this?

Boy: Is that the water?

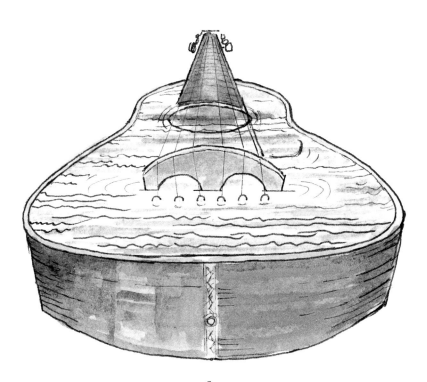

Technique

Boy: I like using my left hand on the guitar
as I never use my left hand for anything else.
He starts picking his nails.
Boy: Apart from picking my nails off.

♫

Regarding Jimi Hendrix:
Boy: We all know he's good,
but we still know I'm better.

Music Theory

Me: What is a crotchet?

Boy: They're the things you walk around with when you've broken your leg.

HOW MANY TIMES
DO I NEED TO TELL YOU -
I AM NOTHING LIKE
ONE OF YOU HASHTAGS!

I point to the sharp sign.

Me: What's that in the key signature of G Major?

Girl: It's got a hashtag.

Me: What's that?

Boy: That's a B blunt.

Me: No! What do I live in?

Boy: Oh, B flat!

Me: The big *f* means play loudly.
What do you think the big *p* means?
Girl: Personal?
Me: What?
Girl: For 'Personal Information'.

♫

Boy: Doesn't *mp* stand for Member of Parliament?

♫

Me: What does *dolce* mean?
Boy: I don't know.
I tell him it means to play sweetly.
Boy: What does Gabbana mean?

Girl points to a note.

Girl: Is that a Walkers?

Me: No, it's a quaver.

Girl: What are the Walkers?

Me: They're crisps.

I point to a note.

Me: What's this note called?

Boy: Baby.

Me: Baby?

Boy: It's a good name.

Scales

Me: Please play the C major scale.
Boy: You mean the scale of C major?

Me: You need to learn your scales.
Boy: My tiny brain can't learn them.
I've used up all my memory learning
all my Transformers' names.
I have lots of them.

After playing the melodic minor scale:

Boy: It's stressful.

Me: Stressful?

Boy: Yeah, it can't make up its mind what it wants to do.

Chords

Boy: I really, really love the E minor chord.

Is there an adult version?

Me: Err... E major?

Boy refuses to play D/F# chord.

Me: So, when you come to face challenges in life
you won't try and overcome them?
You'll come across more challenging things
than a D/F# chord.

Boy: Nothing's going to be worse than a D/F# chord.

♫

Me: Why do you keep on playing a B7 chord when you're
supposed to play E?

Boy: I don't think it's fair on B7 as there are loads of E
chords and only two bars of B7.

Me: Well I'm sure B7 is really grateful that you're
sticking up for it, but you really should play an E chord
there, otherwise it's a completely different song.

Boy: I just don't think it's fair.

Listening Tests

I play through the short piece used for the Grade 1 listening test.
Boy interrupts in the middle of the test.

Boy: Don't you feel sorry for the person
who wrote this song?

Me: Why?

Boy: It's being used for a test.

Me: The music is written specifically for these tests.

Boy: Oh! Did they get paid?

Me: I'm going to play the melody once.

Tell me if the last note is higher or lower than the first note.

I play a short melody.

Boy: Lower.

Me: Well done! Now I'm going to play the same piece again, twice. Raise your hand when you hear a rhythm or pitch change on the second time.

Boy raises his hand at the correct moment.

Me: Great! That's an improvement on last week.

Boy: I remembered the answers from last week.

Me: What?

Boy: I remembered where to put my hand up.

Me: But they're different pieces.

Singing

Boy: Singing is singing.

It's not music.

♫

Boy: What are you doing?

Me: I'm singing along with your playing.

Boy: Please don't.

Me: I get paid to sing I'll have you know.

Boy: Don't be stupid.

Girl: I think I'm good at singing but my sisters say I'm not.

But when they say it again, I have a good comeback.

Me: What's that?

Girl: You're not good at singing either...

But at home, I have better things to say.

I have a whole book of comebacks - 200 of them.

I've used around 50 and crossed them off.

Musical Meanderings & Off Topic Conversations

Boy: Do elves play the electric guitar?

Me: This is a song by the band Oasis.

They're from Manchester.

Have you been to Manchester?

Boy has a blank look on his face.

Me: It's in the north.

Boy: Is it north of Dulwich?

Boy: My brother loves Oasis,

but I don't know if he means the drink or the band.

Me: Did your sister get into your school?

Boy: No, she's going to [the name of his sister's school].

Me: Is that a boarding school?

Boy: Yes. It's a girls' school.

I was gutted not to get in.

♫

Girl describes how terrible she thought her classmate's

Secret Santa present was.

Me: Why don't you try and be nice to each other?

Girl: Nice? I'm in a girls' school.

♫

Me: Did you like that Louis Armstrong video?

Boy: Yes. Is Neil Armstrong his father?

Boy looks at my timetable.

Boy: You have a pupil called 'Lunch'?

♫

After hearing that his friend is learning a song by rock band
Arctic Monkeys:

Boy: Isn't Charlie playing something
by the Arctic Penguins?

♫

Boy: What happens in *A Star is Born?*
Is someone born and they're called Star?

Me: Do you like Science?

Girl: I was born to do Science.

Girl: I'm really dyslexic but I know what 14 x 2 is.

Me: What is it?

Girl: I can't remember.

Boy explains why children don't get tired on Christmas Day,
even after waking early.

Boy: There's something called Christmas-energy.
It's a known thing and all children have it.

♫

Me: You're not in Jesus Christ Superstar?
Boy: Thankfully not.
Those things are public humiliation.

♫

Me: Your tie looks awful; you need to do it properly.
Boy: No.
Me: What if the headmaster sees you?
Boy: I'll say I'm John the Baptist
who only cares about one thing
and that is my guitar lesson and not my clothes.

Boy: Some people have corrupted souls.

Not everyone can be nice though.

♫

Regarding naughty boys:

Boy: Their souls are too filled with darkness

to be filled with music.

Me: Do you know what 'having the blues' means?

Boy: I think it's a type of cold.

Me: Have you heard of a 'one-hit wonder'?

Boy: Yes. It's almost like a hole-in-one, but for songs.

Boy: I know what humans can't do –
they can't break concrete with their heads.

Girl mentions The Sound of Music.

Me: When I was your age, I wanted to be Marta and my sister wanted to be Gretel.

Girl: I want to be Kurt.

Girl: I love going to Burnley to see my grandparents. You can do *crazy* things in Burnley.

Me: Like what?

Girl: Like walking in public with underwear on my head!

Me: *Errr...*

Girl: And putting makeup all over my grandparents' bed... Yeah, you can do anything in Burnley.

Boy: They don't look like drummers on that poster up there.

Me: What do drummers look like?

Boy: They have long hair, whitish blackish skin, funny hats and raggy clothes.

Joint Lessons with Twins

Girl 2: You're pulling that face again.
The one where you're stopping
yourself from laughing.
Girl 1: It's a good thing,
as I've stopped myself from laughing.

G1: What was your worst year of school?
Me: I liked school actually and don't have one.
G1: What?! Is that because you hated your parents'?
Followed by an 'I think I've crossed the line'
facial expression.

G2: I knew it was you doing that voice
when we were on holiday that time!
You told me I had voices in my head!

After bickering for some time, G2 looks upset.

G1: Treat others how you would like to be treated –
I treat you rude, so you treat me rude.

Me: You two are bickering again.
I think you really love bickering.
G1: Oh yes, we do!
We really want to go to therapy.

History

A boy flicks through the Grade 1 rock guitar
examination syllabus.

Boy: There's one by the World Health Organisation.

Me: The Who!

♫

Boy: When was *Take Me Home, Country Roads* written?

Me: The 70s.

Boy: The 17th century?

♫

Boy: 1994. That's before pop, right?

Boy: I love 80s music.

Me: What are you listening to at the moment?

Boy: Nirvana.

Me: That's more 90s.

Boy: 70s, 80s, 90s, it's all the same thing.

♫

During two different lessons on the same day, I ask each student if they can name the members of The Beatles. I'm greeted with two blank faces, then the same hopeful guess from each:

Keith Lemon?

[Help!]

School Parties

Boy: Marble parties were better than dot parties.*

Me: You had a party and played with marbles?

Boy: No!

Me: What was a marble party?

Boy: Every time we did something good,

we were given a marble and then we put it in a jar.

Once the jar was full, we had a party.

Me: And played with the marbles?

Boy: No, why would we do that?

We had drinks and played games and watched films.

Dot parties are exactly the same as Marble Jar parties,
except with dots (i.e. stickers) instead of marbles.

Boy: We used to have Marble Jar parties in Year 2.

That was three years ago.

Now my childhood's dead.

School Trips

In 2017:

Me: Are you looking forward to the school trip?

Boy: Yes, but I think I look forward more to coming back.

♫

The same boy in 2020:

Me: How was the trip to Wales last week?

Boy: Good.

Later on, when packing up his guitar:

Me: What was the best bit of Wales then?

Boy: Going home.

Me: How was the trip to the Buddhist Centre?

Girl: It was OK.

Two hours of talking and then half an hour
of meditation.

Me: How was the meditating?

Girl: It was stressful.

Birthdays

Boy: I don't like art.

The only good thing about it

is that a famous artist died on my birthday.

Me: Who?

Boy: Paul Klee. He died 70 years before I was born.

Me: That's the only good thing about art?

Boy: Yes.

♫

Girl: I have a good memory.

I remember when I was born.

It was my birthday.

♫

Me: What are you doing for your birthday?

Girl: I want to watch Cats.

I've never in my life seen a talking cat.

The Mind of a Boy

After telling him he played really well:

Boy: Thinking about conspiracy theories calms my mind.

Boy: I have VR now.

Me: Virtual reality?

Boy: No, Verbal Reasoning.

When I first saw VR in my timetable,

I thought it might be virtual reality.

but then I looked at my English teacher

and I knew that was a 'no'.

I don't even think he would know

how to work a VR system.

Or a computer.

Or anything in the 21st century.

Me: What are your favourite lessons at school?

Boy: Break or lunch. They're in a time period,

so they count as lessons!

Me: Do you like doing stand-up comedy?

Boy: Yes, but I prefer to sit down.

♫

After collecting a boy from his French class:

Me: All your French teachers are actually French.

Boy: They could have gone to accent-changing lessons?

Me: You don't think they're really French?

Boy: 10 percent no, but probably yes.

I wouldn't change my accent now,

but it's something I would do when I'm a teenager.

I would change it to American

and then regret it later on in life.

Me: I used to teach that gap year student.

Maybe you'll come back as a gap student.

Boy: No, I probably won't.

And anyway, you'll be retired by then.

♪♩

Boy: It makes me upset when it says in the Latin book

'blank page', but it's not a blank page

if it has writing on it.

♪♩

Boy: You know when you lean against a car door

and you fall out?

Me: No, I haven't had that.

Boy: Well I hit the kerb.

Luckily, I was going to the hospital anyway.

blank page

Concentrate Please!

Boy stops playing in the middle of a song.

Boy: Why can't I stop thinking about
my rabbit, Snuggles?

Boy: Sometimes I wonder how much school knows about me?

Me: What do you mean?

Boy: I mean, do they know about my pets?

♫

Me: Start the song now.

Boy: Wait, I'm thinking about something.

Me: What's that?

Boy: I'm hoping my rabbit isn't dead.

♫

Me: Here's a challenge: try to play a whole song without talking.

Boy: Sometimes I stop breathing if I'm not allowed to talk.

Girl: Do you know what I'm thinking about?

Me: No.

Girl: My two dead fish.

♫

Me: Remember when we played the
'New World Theme'?

Boy: Yes.

Me: Have you seen the Hovis bread advert?

Boy: Yes.

Me: Well the song on that is the 'New World Theme'.

Boy: Oh right. I've seen an advert for bagels too.

♫

Regarding the song 'Aunt Rhody':

Boy: Who would make up a song about their Aunt?

Me: Let's look at where it says 'Daily Scales'.

Boy: Is that like a newspaper for musicians? Bah-dum-tish!

Groups and Bands

Boy: What's Cello Club?

Me: What it says on the tin.

Boy: That's a rubbish name for a club.

♪

Me: Please can you be my guinea pig
for the new guitar group piece?

Ten minutes later.

Boy: Where's the guinea pig? In your pocket?

Year 7 Rock Band is rehearsing.

Me to the drummer (Boy 1): Why did you stop playing in the middle of the song?

Boy 1: I twisted my foot on the foot pedal and it really hurts.

Boy 2: Shall I give it a massage for you?

Boy 1: Yes please.

Boy 2 walks over and promptly starts massaging said foot.

Practising

Boy: I left my guitar at school,
so I didn't have it at home...
but I did really good
air guitar practice this week.

Girl: I couldn't practise this week
as I was opening presents.

Me: Do you watch TV?

Girl: Yes, far too much.

Me: Well, why don't you practise first,
before watching TV?

Girl: Oh no, I don't think I'll be able to do that
as I'm addicted to television.

Regarding a song called 'Needing a Rest':

Boy: I like 'Needing a Rest'.

Sometimes I use the four-beat rest to have a lie down.

More from the same lethargic boy:

Me: How many ledger lines does this note have?

Boy (with a sigh): It's not a very 'leisure-ful' note. You can't lie down.

Music Therapy

Boy is struggling with a piece.

Me: That's it, you can do it.

Boy: Are you a guitar teacher or a self-motivator?

♫

Year 6 boy finishes dancing to 'Eye of the Tiger'.

Boy: I think that's the biggest smile I've had since Year 2.

♫

After playing through the James Bond Theme for the first time:

Boy: That felt so good!

It's almost as good as KK Bubblegum!*

*No, I have no idea either.

About Yours Truly

Boy: I see you're having a bad hair day.

♫

Girl: What did you do for fun when you were little?
Because you probably didn't have
electricity then and iPads.

♫

Girl: You're dressed like Cinderella when she's a maid.

Lockdown Lessons

Boy: I've been chatting to my "friends".

He does air-quotes with his fingers.

Me: What does that mean?

Boy: My girlfriends.

Me: How many do you have?

Boy: I have no idea.

♫

The iPad drops during the online lesson.

Boy: Oh no!

My mummy won't be happy if this breaks

as this costs a billion or a million pounds

and I don't have a billion pounds

to buy a new one.

I hear "F*** me!" in the background.

Girl: Did you hear that?

Me: No.

Girl: My Daddy swored.

(Another expletive in the distance).

Girl: He's swored again!

♪

Boy: All my technology is going wrong.
I had a horrible Maths lesson with a potato filter on
and I didn't even realise.*

Image used with kind permission of Phillip Walton at Lens Studio

School Trips, Lockdown Edition

Yes, it's that boy again – see page 39.

Boy: The Year 8s are missing some of the
best trips when most of them
usually involve a lot of pain.

♫

A different boy laments a cancelled school trip.

Boy: We've missed the best trip this year.

Me: Where were you supposed to be going?

Boy: York.

Me: Why is York the *best* trip?

Boy: Because we would have been allowed to go to
McDonalds on our own.

The Lifting of Lockdown

Boy: I'm really mediocre size.
I don't want to be a giant or a titch.
That's my least favourite part about going back to school:
seeing if my clothes and shoes still fit.

♫

Girl: After lockdown I'm going to Harry Potter World
and I'm going to get a wand.
I'm not going to get a broom because I don't
think it will work.
I asked my Dad how much a wand will be and he said
he didn't know but I could just find a stick.

End of the Lesson

Boy: Is it possible for me to get a Distinction
for all my grades?
Me: Anything is possible.
Boy: Flying isn't.

♫

Boy inspects the minor marks on his guitar.
Boy: My guitar has been bonked
in every place imaginable...
That should be a piece,
"bonk, bonk, bonk..."

Me: What are you doing for the rest of the day?

Boy: I'm going to see The Hundred.

Me: Is that a film or a band?

Boy: It's cricket.

As a student is leaving the room:

Boy: When I eat too much gluten,
my butt gets sticky when things come out.
That's too much information isn't it?

Me: Yes. Bye!

In no particular order...

Jamie Ogilvie-Forbes

Dan Frost   Penny Price

Toby Stockdale   Richard Simmons

Debbie McLean   Tanya Brooman

Ruth Simmons   John Stockdale

Katy Stockdale   Mark Sinker

THANK YOU

Suki johal   Phil Walton

Angela McMahon   Sheena Vachhani   Melinda Wells

And the parents of my students for your encouragement and enthusiam for this project.